The Gift of Speaking in Tongues

The Holy Spirit, the Human Spirit and the Gift of Holy Speech

Mark J Cartledge

Lecturer in Christian Theology,
University of Wales at Lampeter

GROVE BOOKS LIMITED
RIDLEY HALL RD CAMBRIDGE CB3 9HU

Contents

The Cover Illustration depicts the day of Pentecost

First Impression January 2005
ISSN 1470-8531
ISBN 1 85174 583 1

Introduction 1

In the autumn of 1979 I attended a house meeting that was organized by members of the church. It was an occasion for young people to listen to a visiting speaker and about 15 of us crammed into the lounge to hear what the speaker had to say. After 25 years I cannot actually remember anything about the message, but I do remember what happened after he stopped speaking. We were invited to receive the baptism in the Holy Spirit and so we prayed together. It was during this occasion that I had an overwhelming sense of the presence of God accompanied by such joy that I could not stop laughing. As I laughed and prayed I also discovered that strange sounds began to come unexpectedly out of my mouth. I uttered the first faltering sounds of what I learned to call the gift of speaking in tongues. What is more, I was the only person in the room to do so and it was embarrassing to say the least—everyone was watching me! Ever since that day I have been interested in the gift, and in the following years I have attempted to understand it better for my own spiritual life and the benefit of others. I have had many questions and some of them remain with me since they are only partially answered. However, it is hoped that some of your own questions will be addressed adequately, as well as new ones clarified, as you read this booklet.

The Pentecostal and charismatic movements of the last 100 years or so have been associated with one spiritual gift in particular—speaking in tongues, otherwise known as glossolalia. There are famous landmarks in the history of the gift within Pentecostal history. These include the watchnight service on 31 December 1900 at Charles Fox Parham's Bible School in Topeka, Kansas. A woman by the name of Agnes Ozman asked Parham to lay his hands upon her head and pray for the baptism in the Holy Spirit as evidenced by the gift of speaking in tongues. It was subsequent to this prayer that Ozman was reported to have spoken in tongues for the very first time. It was consequently regarded as a sign of the baptism of the Holy Spirit. The Welsh Revival of 1904 was reported to have manifested the gift, and it was said to have occurred in 1905 by missionaries in India. However, the most significant outbreak of speaking in tongues occurred in Los Angeles in April 1906 when a revivalist group led by the preacher, William Seymour, experienced what came to be called the Azusa Street Revival, often associated with the birth of Pentecostalism.

Subsequently, the fire of revival bringing the baptism of the Spirit and the gift of speaking in tongues spread throughout the USA, Europe and many parts of the world.

In the early 1960s the gift of speaking in tongues was experienced in what were considered at the time to be more mainstream denominations, such as Anglican, Baptist and Methodist. Famously the American Episcopalian Rector, Dennis Bennett, was forced to resign when he admitted from the pulpit that he had been baptized in the Spirit and received the gift of speaking in tongues. However, the renewal movement soon spread and by 1967 the Roman Catholic charismatic renewal could be added to the list of hitherto Protestant groups. During this period, a number of key proponents of the renewal movement were in fact neo-Pentecostals, that is, they accepted the Pentecostal doctrine of baptism in the Spirit as a second post-conversion experience evidenced by speaking in tongues. However, this was to change in the 1980s with the influence of John Wimber and the Vineyard movement, also called the Third Wave (Pentecostals being the first wave and 1960s–1970s renewalists the second). Wimber and many of his colleagues denied the two-stage process of Pentecostalism, believing the Spirit was received at conversion. This meant that they also relativized the gift of tongues. It was simply one gift among many, but what became more in focus were signs and wonders, including words of knowledge and healing.

Recent studies have given greater insight into the nature and function of the gift

Academically, there is a vast amount of research on the subject of speaking in tongues, especially from the 1970s and 1980s. It has been studied from New Testament, historical, theological, sociological, psychological and linguistic perspectives. But only recently has the gift been given fresh attention and it is some of these more recent studies from within Pentecostalism, as well as from social science, that have given greater insight into the nature and function of the gift.

This Grove booklet does not aim to break new ground but to make accessible some of the insights of this research. It is written with an eye to enable churches and Christians to appreciate recent thinking on the subject and to deal with the important questions for today. So, the questions that will guide me include:

- What exactly is the gift of speaking in tongues?
- Is it really a gift of the Holy Spirit?
- Is it human languages?
- In what way is it a language of angels?

- Does it signify baptism in the Spirit?
- How does it relate to the human spirit?
- How should it be used today?
- What are the problems associated with its use?

These are all important questions for the contemporary church engaged in renewal. As can be seen, this study is embarking on a well-trodden path and therefore I do not claim (as other Grove booklets do) to write the 'first word,' but I can aim to write a 'different word.' I intend to share my own understanding and hope that others with different insights might be able to engage in a conversation with my position. It is offered in the anticipation that it might be encouraging and beneficial. It is a position that has been shaped by research and by ongoing thinking and writing, as well as by experience and the practice of Christian ministry.

2   The Gift in the New Testament: An Overview

In the New Testament there are 35 references to the phrase 'speaking in tongues.'

The majority of these references occur in 1 Corinthians, of which 23 appear in chapter 14. The remaining 7 occurrences are in the longer ending to the Gospel of Mark and the Acts of the Apostles. The main phrase that is used to refer to the gift is literally 'tongues to speak,' translated 'speaking in tongues.' Occasionally there are slight differences: 'to speak in a tongue' or 'to speak (in) other tongues.' The longer ending (see below) of Mark alone says that 'they will speak in new tongues.'

The Longer Ending of Mark

In Mark's gospel the reference to speaking in new tongues comes in the passage at the end of the gospel that is often called the longer ending. This longer ending is usually regarded as an addition to the original manuscript. Nevertheless, it provides some important insight into the mission of the early church and the role of the gift of tongues. In this section of the gospel the context is a resurrection appearance and commission to the disciples to preach the good news. Associated with this gospel commission is the mandate to drive out demons, speak in new tongues, pick up snakes, drink poison and heal the sick. Thus speaking in tongues in this context is associated with the ongoing mission of the disciples to spread the gospel by word and deed.

The Acts of the Apostles

In the Acts of the Apostles, the appearance of the gift is associated with the day of Pentecost itself (2.1–4). In the upper room, the Holy Spirit descends on the disciples in 'tongues of fire' and they begin 'to speak in other tongues.' The onlookers are able to hear their own languages and are duly astounded. Luke records that the hearers are amazed that they can hear the disciples 'declaring the wonders of God' in their own languages and dialects. This is a cause of amazement and, of course, also a cause of mocking. Peter famously declares that these disciples are not drunk, as some supposed, because 'it is only nine o'clock in the morning.' Later in Acts, Luke records an outbreak of such speaking in 10.44 when Peter is recorded to have visited the Gentile household of Cornelius. As Peter speaks the Holy Spirit is outpoured upon the company and the Gentiles receive the gift of the Spirit, speak in tongues and praise God. In 19.2 the Ephesian disciples of John hear the good news of Jesus Christ and are baptized into his name. Paul subsequently lays his hands upon them and they speak in tongues and prophesy.

Thus in the Acts of the Apostles the gift of tongues is associated with the giving of the Holy Spirit in power to the Jews and the Gentiles, the declaration of the wonders of God, otherwise known as praise, the prayer of Paul with the laying on of his hands, and the gift of prophecy.

Paul's First Epistle to the Corinthians

The most information, as the number of references indicates, can be found in Paul's first letter to the Corinthians. In 12.10 Paul mentions 'speaking in different kinds of tongues' as well as the complementary gift of 'the interpretation of tongues.' In the context of this passage Paul uses the metaphor of body to refer to the church. Each person, like a part of the body, has gifts to be used for the common good. Therefore only some 'speak in different kinds of tongues,' whilst others interpret what is being said in the assembly. However, Paul would prefer that all the believers demonstrate love in their lives rather than speak in tongues, whether the speech is human or angelic.

While this is beneficial for the person concerned he would prefer that in the assembly intelligible words dominate

In chapter 14 Paul considers the gift in the greatest detail anywhere to be found in the New Testament. He states that tongues speech is directed primarily to God and therefore can appear to be incomprehensible to human hearers. He calls this speech 'mysteries in the Spirit.' They benefit the assembled people when they are understood and appreciated as containing revelation or communication from God. For this to occur, if anyone feels compelled to speak, they should also pray for the gift of interpretation so that they can explain the meaning of the speech to the others present. Paul speaks of praying in tongues as 'praying in the spirit,' that is, in a way that bypasses the mind, hence he is able to say that the mind is unfruitful. And while this is beneficial for the person concerned he would prefer that in the assembly intelligible words dominate because tongues speech can be either not interpreted or misinterpreted. Say, for example, that an unbeliever enters the church assembly and discovers all the Christians present babbling away in unknown languages with no one knowing what is going on, they would be scandalized, thinking that everyone is mad. In order to stop this wrong impression there should be some kind of order with only a few people speaking a public message, perhaps two or three at the most and then separately. These speeches should be interpreted by those with the gift of interpretation and others should 'weigh' them to discern whether what is said is from God. Then all the assembly can be encouraged in their faith and the conduct of worship will be orderly.

Summary

The New Testament evidence gives us some idea as to what the writers regarded the gift to be. For the longer ending of Mark, it was a sign that should be used to accompany the proclamation of the gospel. It is only one sign among many and the text does not tell us much more than this. It has a positive symbolic role in drawing attention to the proclamation of the gospel. For Luke, the gift is associated with the overwhelming presence of the Holy Spirit and especially praise, which is itself an aspect of prophecy. Clearly, for Luke, the miraculous dimension of the gift is that of speech, as the disciples actually use their own speech organs to praise God in an inspired way. It is not that the hearers have been inspired to hear, but the speakers to speak, and in 'other' languages, that is, real human languages not otherwise known. It is not entirely clear if that is what is envisaged in Acts 10 and 19 but it is fair to presume that Luke's understanding as expressed in Acts 2 would undergird the rest of the book.

For Paul it is a gift that can be used to edify the spirit even as the mind is bypassed

For Paul, we encounter a slightly different scenario. Speaking in tongues is certainly symbolic of an encounter with the Holy Spirit but not quite in the same way as for Luke. For Paul it is associated with the human spirit praying in and with the Holy Spirit so that mysteries are expressed to God. It is a gift that can be used to edify the spirit even as the mind is bypassed. However, in the assembly, order must prevail and those people who are abusing the gift must be controlled for the benefit of all, hence the need for the speech to be interpreted and become intelligible if a revelation is to be disclosed. Elsewhere, Paul speaks of the Spirit at work in the disciples as a groaning or longing for the consummation of the kingdom of God (Romans 8.26). Many Pentecostals and charismatic Christians have considered this to be an allusion to the gift of speaking in tongues. It certainly resonates with the material contained in 1 Corinthians 14.

It is probably fair to say that these different writers all consider the gift of tongues to be a signifier of the spiritual life — as symbolic of the gospel proclamation, or of the overwhelming presence of the Holy Spirit and prophetic praise, or of the mysterious dimensions of prayer and revelation.

The Linguistic Nature of Tongues

The linguistic nature of the gift of tongues has been a cause of considerable debate. It is certainly clear from the narrative of the Acts of the Apostles that Luke considered the gift to be real human languages ('foreign speech,' *xenolalia*). It is probable that Paul also considered the speech to be primarily real human speech (hence, language of 'men' in 1 Cor 13 NIV) although he supplements it with another category, namely the language of angels. This second linguistic category is itself quite a mystery and despite the best efforts of scholars it is simply unclear. Paul, it is thought, considered there to be a range of angelic languages that mirror human speech and that tongues of the spirit inspired by the Holy Spirit could include languages from this realm. Some Pentecostals have made a lot of this, but it would be unwise to speculate too much.

Contemporary examples of tongues speech have been examined by scholars and the evidence is often considered to be weak and difficult to interpret. In many cases there is simply insufficient material properly recorded and for a sufficient length of time. However, there is considerable anecdotal evidence of people speaking in real and unlearned human languages, but this has not been studied more thoroughly. Some people regard the contemporary phenomenon to be largely 'nonsense' language that conveys meaning through mood and tone rather than through 'words.' Others suggest that it shares certain characteristics of

What can be said is that linguistically there is still a sense of uncertainty surrounding the phenomenon

language and at the same time contains some unique features than are unlike language. What can be said is that linguistically there is still a sense of uncertainty surrounding the phenomenon. On rare occasions it may be the case that a real unlearned human language is spoken. However, for the most part it is a language that defies current linguistic theory and simply cannot be pinned down with precision. This means that we should avoid dogmatism on this matter and learn to live with the mystery.

Questions for Reflection

- In what ways might the perspectives of Luke and Paul be combined?

- How does this summary of the biblical material compare with the teaching you have received on the gift of speaking in tongues?

3

The Purpose of the Gift

What exactly is the purpose of speaking in tongues?

Classical Pentecostalism answers this question by differentiating between the sign of tongues and the gift of tongues.

The Sign of Tongues

As I have already mentioned, the sign of tongues is seen by some to refer to its role as evidence of someone having received the second blessing, otherwise known as the baptism in the Spirit. In Pentecostal theology this dramatic experience of grace is subsequent to conversion and is an empowerment for Christian witness in mission. Thus tongues signify that a person has received the fullness of the Christian life by such an empowerment since they have been overwhelmed by the Spirit as on the day of Pentecost.

The case made for this position is based on the narrative of the Acts of the Apostles. In Acts 2.1–4 we read how the disciples of Jesus were altogether in one place when a violent wind filled the house and a vision of fiery tongues came to rest on each of them. They were all filled with the Holy Spirit and began to speak in other tongues as the Spirit enabled them. Thus there is a strong correlation between the Holy Spirit filling the disciples and the evidence of such filling by them speaking in other tongues. This is regarded as the fulfilment of the promise earlier in Acts 1.8 when Jesus said 'you will receive power when the Holy Spirit comes on you; and you will be my witnesses…' This is regarded as a norm in the spiritual life of Christians and should be an expectation for all in Christ.

This norm is then understood to be in evidence on other occasions in the book of Acts. In Acts 10.46 at the house of Cornelius the Gentile, when Peter was still speaking the Holy Spirit came upon the hearers of the message and they spoke in tongues and praised God. This caused astonishment that Gentiles could also receive the gift of the Spirit and it opened the way to them being baptized in water, since they had already been baptized in the Spirit. Also, in Acts 19.6 when Paul placed his hands on the disciples of John at Ephesus we read that the Holy Spirit came upon them and they spoke in tongues and prophesied. It is also assumed by Pentecostals that Acts 8.17 describing the reception of Spirit by the Samaritans includes the sign of tongues but this is not explicit. In fact it provides an important counter example within the book of Acts where the Spirit is received in dramatic fashion and the sign of tongues is not in evidence (see also 9.17–18).

It is with these texts from the Acts of the Apostles that classical Pentecostal denominations defined the importance of speaking in tongues as the initial sign of baptism in the Holy Spirit. The exact phrasing of this doctrine varies between the different Pentecostal denominations, with some American definitions using the phrase 'physical evidence.' Some Pentecostal denominations regard it as the only sign, while others might see it as primary but nevertheless allow different signs such as prophecy to function in a similar manner. To illustrate the doctrine here is a quotation from the 'Statement of Fundamental Truths of the Assemblies of God' in the USA:

> *#8: The Initial Physical Evidence of the Baptism in the Holy Ghost.* The baptism of believers in the Holy Ghost is witnessed by the initial physical sign of speaking with other tongues as the Spirit of God gives them utterance (Act 2.4). The speaking in tongues in this instance is the same in essence as the gift of tongues (1 Cor 12.4–10, 28), but different in purposes and use.[1]

The sign value of tongues is relatively clear from the classical Pentecostal tradition. Of course, there is the difficult passage in 1 Corinthians 14.20–25 to interpret, and in particular the idea that tongues are 'a sign for unbelievers,' while prophecy is a 'sign for believers.' Classical Pentecostal interpreters such as Harold Horton argue that the context of this statement is the worship meeting for believers. If an unbeliever hears this 'sign' they mock because they do not understand its significance, therefore it becomes to them a sign of judgment. In fact, the word 'sign' here can mean either a sign of judgment or a sign of blessing. In the passage Paul cites Isaiah 28.11 to mean that since Israel did not listen to God when he spoke through the prophets, now he will speak through the foreign language of an invading army. This is used by Paul to mean that tongues without interpretation is a sign of judgment because once again God is speaking in incomprehensible language. Prophecy, however, is understood as God revealing himself to his people and as such is a sign of blessing.

The Gift of Tongues

In Pentecostal theology the gift of tongues differs only in so far as it amounts to the use of the gift subsequent to its initial reception. That is, whenever tongues is used in prayer, praise and prophecy (when accompanied by an interpretation) after the initial use, then it is the gift rather than the sign. There are many classical Pentecostals who have only ever spoken in tongues at their baptism in the Spirit, for they subsequently never used the gift.

In the charismatic renewal movement this doctrine was never held in any official sense. In the 1960s Michael Harper came very close to accepting this doctrine, since he regarded it as a 'normal accompaniment' and 'the sign of this blessing.'[2] By the mid 1970s he had changed his position and is not so sure it must always accompany the blessing.[3] In general the charismatic renewal movement has rejected the idea of the sign of tongues, especially as initial evidence, but accepted the gift of tongues within the broader domain of charismatic spirituality.

In the context of charismatic spirituality it is understood to function as a language of prayer and praise. As a spiritual discipline it can enable the believer to become more aware of the presence of God and can be associated with spontaneity in prayer. When sung it has an aesthetic quality resonant with other forms of Christian spiritual expression such as chant and the 'Jesus prayer.'[4] It can liberate the human spirit to praise God and frees the believer from inhibitions in prayer. Paradoxically, tongues transcend language as well as being a mode of speech. In the use of speaking in tongues, language is broken and yet the person is made whole—tongues can be deeply cathartic. Ultimately speaking in tongues can bring intimacy with God and an empowerment in the Christian life. It is these two primary functions that give purpose to the gift within the spirituality of the individual and as expressed within the church. Such intimacy and empowerment brings edification and transformation. It is these functions that lie at the heart of charismatic spirituality.

Ultimately speaking in tongues can bring intimacy with God and an empowerment in the Christian life

The Interpretation of Tongues

The use of the gift of the interpretation of tongues is mentioned by Paul in 1 Corinthians 12.10 and commented on in 14.13–17. He writes:

> For this reason [*ie* edification of the church] anyone who speaks in a tongue should pray that he may interpret what he says. For if I pray in a tongue, my spirit prays but my mind is unfruitful. So what shall I do? I will pray with my spirit, but I will also pray with my mind; I will sing with my spirit, but I will also sing with my mind. If you are praising God with your spirit, how can one who finds himself among those who do not understand say 'Amen' to your thanksgiving, since he does not know what you are saying? You may be giving thanks well enough, but the other person is not edified. (NIV)

In the light of this text, Pentecostals and charismatics have understood that the gift of interpretation within the assembly is exercised for the edification of those present. It is often not understood as a word-for-word 'translation' of the original message, but rather it is a 'declaration of meaning.'

There is a debate in Pentecostal and charismatic circles regarding the direction of the tongues speech in this instance. Is it directed towards God, as in praise and prayer, or is it directed towards the assembly, as in a prophecy from the Lord? From what Paul states it seems likely that what he had in mind was prayer and praise, including thanksgiving. When this is interpreted then others could affirm such a contribution by saying 'Amen,' and thus the congregation is edified. However, by extension such a prayer could contain a prophetic dimension and while this is not the focus of Paul's statement it cannot be ruled out of bounds.

In 14.27–32 Paul indicates that the exercise of word gifts, such as instruction, revelation, tongues or interpretation, should be used to edify the church. He instructs that two or three should speak in tongues at any one time and that someone should interpret. If it is known that no one with the gift of interpretation is present then the tongues speakers should remain quiet and speak to themselves and God. The others in the assembly should weigh what is said. No one must be considered to be out of control for the 'spirits of the prophets are subject to the prophets' (v 32). Of course, this passage needs to be understood within the context of the church at Corinth. There the gift of speaking in tongues had become a badge of super-spiritual status and it was being used without any control whatsoever. It had become a focus of division, which is why Paul devotes so much space to it in his letter. As we interpret this passage today there is clearly a very different context to the one Paul was addressing. I would suggest that the principles of edification and order prevail. There must be some control and at the same time the value of the gift must be affirmed. It is up to each leadership team to work out in prayer and faith how this gift should be used within the public assembly based upon these twin biblical principles.

Questions for Reflection

- How do you understand the relationship between the sign and the gift of tongues? Do you think that the classical Pentecostals are correct? Why (not)?

- Have you heard any interpretations of speaking in tongues? If so, would you compare this speech with contemporary prophecy? Why (not)?

4

A Gift within
Charismatic Spirituality

A charismatic understanding of the phenomenon of speaking in tongues will certainly want to define it as 'gift.'

That is, it is something which is given graciously by and through the Holy Spirit who is at work in us enabling this gift to be used. It is a gift that is given to us by the Spirit and we use it in relation to the human spirit rather than the mind. It has a mysterious and trans-rational quality that defies neat boxes of categorizations and precision of definition. It cannot be pinned down because fundamentally it is about the Holy Spirit and the human spirit. In a number of the references to the use of the gift in 1 Corinthians 14 it cannot be stated with precision whether Paul is talking of the Holy Spirit or the human spirit because they intersect in the use of this gift. This is illustrated by Gordon Fee where he uses the denotation S/spirit to make this precise point. He says with reference to 1 Corinthians 14.14–15: 'Thus he means "my S/spirit prays/sings" in the sense that his own spirit is worshipping, but this transpires by the direct influence of the indwelling Spirit of God.'[5] He also makes a similar point in a much fuller way when he discusses Romans 8.26.[6] In this text he sees Paul as referring to speaking in tongues in the context of intercession. Here the Holy Spirit is united with our spirit as all of creation longs for the liberation of the kingdom of God. These texts give us an indication as to how we might understand the gift as inspired speech in relation to both human speech and speech inspired by the Holy Spirit—in other words, how such speech can be both human and holy, set apart for the glory of God.

It cannot be pinned down because fundamentally it is about the Holy Spirit and the human spirit

Speaking in Tongues and Charismatic Spirituality

The gift of such holy speech is to be located first and foremost within a process of charismatic spirituality. This process can be defined as a search for God, an encounter with Christ by the Spirit and a transformation of the believer. It is an encounter with the Spirit of life, the one who enables speech, for the sake of the purposes of God in the world. This process can be illustrated, for example, by reference to church interiors. If you walk into a church building and you see clearly that the 'altar' is the centre-piece of the furniture then you know that the sacrament of the Eucharist is at the centre, it is a catholic or sacrament-centred spirituality. If you discover that the pulpit or lectern is at the centre, then it is a Word-centred spirituality, with an evangelical emphasis on the preaching. If you discover that instead of an altar or a pulpit there is the praise band or the screen with the words of choruses on it, then you have discovered a charismatic church. Of course, the liturgy necessarily interprets the symbols, so you would need to attend a service to be certain that these symbols are indeed being interpreted as I have suggested—but they certainly give you a very big clue.

I believe that the process of charismatic spirituality contains three interrelated phases, and as such the regular encounter with God in prayer and worship acts as a kind of recapitulation of the whole of the spiritual life.

Phase 1—Search

It is praise that provides the initial phase of charismatic spirituality as choruses are sung many times and as the leaders of worship enable the worshippers to lift their hearts to heaven. It is the *sursum corda* of charismatic spirituality. When speaking in tongues is used in this phase it is often

It is often associated with a sense of beauty and awe as the worshippers seek the Lord with all their hearts

associated with a sense of beauty and awe as the worshippers seek the Lord with all their hearts and receive a glimpse of the beauty and transcendence of the Lord. This is why people speaking in tongues in this phase will do so either loudly or quietly in praise as the Holy Spirit enables the human spirit to search for the Lord. The worshipper will go with the flow of the corporate mood of the congregation. Where there are people who have the gift of music as well as the gift of tongues they can act as catalysts to enable this beauty to be displayed in a wonderful confluence of sound as many voices join together in harmony and unison in the praise and wonder of God.

Phase 2—Encounter

It is also in praise that people meet with the God whom they seek. It is often the case that this phase of encounter overlaps with the seeking of God. Sometimes the search for God can be a struggle and this depends on a whole range of factors such as personal mood and issues, as well as the quality of the worship leadership. But at some point in the process there is often a moment or a sacred space of encounter, when the invitation to lift your hearts to heaven has been not only responded to but made real in the worshipping congregation.

At this point the persons engaged in such worship can have a tremendous sense of intimacy with God and a dramatic sense of empowerment.

Intimacy is a wonderful gift and real longing for us all. We need to belong to others and to connect in a deeply personal way. Simon Chan has suggested that the gift of speaking in tongues can be understood as an expression of intimacy between ourselves and God.[7] It is a way of the human spirit engaging in holy speech because of the intimacy of the Holy Spirit. The two pictures that he brings to this idea of intimacy are the lovers and the parent–child relationship. In the picture of two lovers, a special language is created which semantically is nonsense, but which each of the lovers appreciates. It is an 'idiolect' or the 'goo-goo' language of love. It really does not make sense but then it is not supposed to because it is a language of affection, of delight and wonder. In this way it is more like the gasp and the shout rather than a well-articulated and precisely constructed sentence. The second picture is of a young child and a doting parent and it is again a language of intimacy. This time the image refers to the meaningless prattle of the young child as he or she talks incessantly to the parent. The parent does not understand the noises from the child but nods her head in pleasure and delight. The child is communicating affection, security and familiarity and is doing so with absolute abandon. It is the bond of love that takes great delight in such intimacy and values it as worthy of encouragement and protection. Similarly, the Holy Spirit as the bond of love within the Godhead draws believers into the intimate life of the Triune God through such holy and affectionate speech. It does not make a lot of sense, but to push the importance of linguistic semantics is to miss the point! It is in this intimacy that people also sense an empowerment. The Holy Spirit is the divine Spirit and any encounter is bound to have a powerful effect.

Phase 3—Transformation

In the final phase of charismatic spirituality the believer's faith is built up and the person is edified. The consequences of such an intimate and powerful encounter are to be seen in how people use the gift of holy and mysterious speech in this context. It is used with faith for others. Very often it is used in intercession and the human spirit is empowered by the

The child is communicating affection, security and familiarity and is doing so with absolute abandon

Before such an intimate encounter it might have been difficult for people to intercede with commitment and fervo

Holy Spirit groaning on behalf of a broken world. It is the cry for the kingdom of God to be established in power. Before such an intimate encounter it might have been difficult for people to intercede with commitment and fervour; now it is done with great passion for the kingdom. It may be that the gift is used in the context of spiritual warfare. This is the case in some churches where it is viewed as a weapon in the armoury. Personally, I prefer to understand it as a sign of victory over the powers of darkness, but would understand it as also being included in 'all kinds of prayer' in Ephesians 6.18.

This process of search–encounter–transformation is an ongoing cycle and within the spiritual life of the believer it is not necessary to work through each phase within the same worship service. Once this process is part of one's life, it is possible to engage in the phases in more limited ways. In some churches, for example, the use of spiritual gifts may be confined to the charismatic prayer meeting. In the context of a house group, the search and encounter phases may be more limited in scope and duration with the emphasis being upon intercession and the transformation of the world through the transformed faith of the intercessors.

> *This process of search–encounter–transformation is an ongoing cycle*

Questions for Reflection

- Does the model of search–encounter–transformation fit with your own experience of Christian prayer and worship? To what extent does it interpret the process of charismatic spirituality?

- Are there dominant feelings or affections that characterize your experience of speaking in tongues? If so, can you identify them? Would you give them theological significance?

5   A Sacrament of the Kingdom of God

The gift of speaking in tongues can be understood as a sacrament of the kingdom of God. What do I mean by this?

I wish to draw on the understanding of the gift as a sign but not in the classical Pentecostal doctrinal sense. It is here that I am indebted to John Calvin for his understanding of the sacraments. There are two principal sacraments, baptism and the Lord's Supper, but there is also a sense in which the concept of 'sacrament' can be used more widely. He defines a sacrament as 'an outward sign by which the Lord seals on our consciences the promises of his good will towards us in order to sustain the weakness of our faith; and we in turn attest our piety toward him in the presence of the Lord and his angels and before men.'[8] While the inner/outer dualism has its weaknesses it does allow us to speak about interior and exterior dimensions.

Calvin also wished to extend the category of sacrament to include all the signs given by God to enable human beings to be more certain and confident of the truth of his promises. These signs can be distinguished as either natural or miraculous. He cites the OT examples of the rainbow and the tree of life as natural signs, and the miraculous type can be illustrated by Gideon's fleece and the movement of the sundial for Hezekiah. He understands that:

1 Sacraments are preceded by a promise and that they are joined to it as an appendix which confirms and seals the promise.

2 Usually they require preaching in order to produce faith, and

3 they are a seal of God's good will towards us, which sustains and increases our faith.

4 The sacraments, however, properly fulfil their function when the Holy Spirit comes to them and 'by whose power alone hearts are penetrated and affections moved.'

5 In this way sacraments serve our faith before God primarily and only subsequently do they attest to our confession before others.

6 Finally, in them we are offered Christ who is set forth before us and with him the treasures of heavenly grace, but this is received by faith alone.

These six characteristics of the sacraments can be applied to the gift of speaking in tongues in the following ways:

- The promise of the prophet Joel that the Spirit would be poured out on all flesh was fulfilled on the day of Pentecost. As a sign of such fulfilment the disciples spoke in other tongues and declared the praises of God. As a sacrament of the Spirit, speaking in tongues can be understood as a fulfilment of the prophecy of Joel and a sign of the coming of the kingdom of God.

- Such a dramatic event needs explanation. On the day of Pentecost Peter stood up and addressed the crowd and explained the meaning of the sign of tongues to them. Without such an explanation through preaching the signs of the kingdom of God will never be understood correctly. Such phenomena are never self-interpreting because they always need an explanation.

- The consequence of speaking in tongues is the edification of the speaker, and through the gift of interpretation, the hearers. It nourishes faith and builds trust between believers who share this gift.

- The encounter with God through the gift is fundamentally a gift of grace—it cannot be anything else. All attempts at manufacturing the gifts will fail in their ultimate attempts to nurture faith and build up the body of Christ.

- This gift is to be understood primarily as a worship encounter and an act of praise. Its evidential force is only secondary as our piety, to use Calvin's language, is first before God and secondarily before others. This explains why charismatics place the emphasis on the praise and prayer rather than as evidence for the baptism in the Spirit.

- The gift within the Christian life will always have as its focus the person of Jesus Christ, because we approach God through the mediation of Christ by the Spirit. It is Christ who has received the Spirit in order to pour him out at Pentecost (Acts 2.33). Therefore just as believers receive the benefits of Christ as by an instrument of faith, so it is with this gift of speaking in tongues. Without the gift of faith, it cannot be fully appreciated or exercised.

This sacramental nature of the gift of speaking in tongues is therefore to be understood as symbolic of the kingdom of God. Like all sacraments it signifies the in-breaking of the kingdom of God into the here and now. The gift of human speech is given new and transposed significance as it is reconfigured in praise and prayer. In the heavenly kingdom this language will fulfil its *telos*, its End. But in the present age we glimpse something of that future glory amid the groaning of creation. Therefore, while this sacrament does point to the reign of God in the *now* of our experience, it also points to the *not yet*. The sacrament of speaking in tongues not only signifies that the kingdom has come, it also signifies that the kingdom has not yet fully arrived. The sign contains both the now and the not yet, expressed in senses of power and weakness in those who use the gift. The side of vulner-

Like all sacraments it signifies the in-breakir of the kingdom of God into the here and now

ability in the light of the not yet of the kingdom may not be a well-known or acknowledged feature, but it is essential to any theology of the gift as sacrament. The signs of the kingdom of God are broken and temporal signs and will pass away when that which is perfect arrives, namely the consummation of the kingdom of God.

Questions for Reflection

- What is your understanding of a sacrament? Can you apply sacramental theology to the sign value of tongues?

- To what extent do you see speaking in tongues as a symbol of weakness as well as power?

The Practice of Speaking in Tongues 6

There are a number of more practical questions associated with the gift of speaking in tongues.

Like any other gift of the Spirit it is not something that is necessarily for everyone, although many people are able to receive it and use it. Certainly these comments should not be interpreted to mean that *all* should acquire this gift and that it has a normative status. Rather, I wish to suggest that it is within the normal range of gifts within the spiritual life even if has no special status. To give it such status is to begin to fall into the trap the Corinthian tongues speakers seem to have fallen into.

Beginning to Speak in Tongues

There are many different examples of how people have acquired the gift of speaking in tongues. These range from an unsolicited and spontaneous experience, without any prior understanding or awareness of what it is that is happening, to a step by step instruction which is practised in some churches. The fact that there is evidence of two extremes in this matter and quite a bit in between suggests that we have an interplay that can be emphasized differently. Just as the gift itself is a mixed phenomenon, so it contains *both* a divine *and* human dynamic in its acquisition. Certainly it is common for one or more people to pray for others to receive the gift within Pentecostal and charismatic churches. It is inevitable that within such a context certain social-psychological dynamics are at work. It is also the case that aspects of how the beginning of such speech is acquired can depend on the learning environ-

> *Just as the gift itself is a mixed phenomenon, so it contains both a divine and human dynamic in its acquisition*

ment. It can be common to find that within a certain social group a number of individuals have tongues speech that sound quite similar to each other. This is not surprising if they have prayed for each other and with each other. The important point to remember is that however the gift is acquired it is for the edification of the believer and the church and should be directed towards God in worship and in prayer.

The Psychology of Speaking in Tongues

By the 'psychology of speaking in tongues' I do not mean to interpret tongues within psychological theory, although that has been attempted. What I am referring to is the inner mental world and emotions that often accompany such speech. Quite often the thoughts of the worshipper and pray-ers are the same as others engaged in spiritual exercises of one kind or another. Tongues speech, however, is not vacuous but tends to be used in a mentally focused way. In the search phase the thoughts that accompany the speech can be understood in terms of the nature of God, his attributes and provision, together with thankfulness for salvation in Christ and the experience of his presence by the Spirit. In the encounter phase the thoughts of the speaker may turn to adoration and joy. At this point the speech may trip over itself in a superabundance of speech. Alternatively it may run out of steam and end in silence, what may be called an apophatic dimension associated with this kind of speech. In the phase of transformation, there is a renewed purpose and particular needs and intercessory concerns dominate and the person speaking in tongues has these matters at the forefront of his or her mind.

At this point the speech may trip over itself in a superabundance of speech

Speaking in tongues has often been viewed as 'ecstatic' speech and it has been understood by some to have been triggered by a state of trance. (This perception owes something to the NEB translation of tongues as 'ecstatic utterance'—an example of the power of the translator to influence the doctrine of the church!) In my research I found this notion to be largely unfounded with respect to regular use of the gift. There are no unique emotions associated with the gift and no particular emotional state that can be readily identified. In fact, like prayer in general terms, speaking in tongues can be experienced emotionally in a variety of ways. The initial experience of speaking in tongues can, however, be a very heightened emotional experience that is often associated with catharsis.

The Community of Faith

Most of the people who speak in tongues do so because they are part of a group who speak in tongues. For the gift to be sustained and nurtured there needs to be a community of faith that allows for the gift to be expressed both publicly and privately. In public it may be via the use of singing in tongues during worship or by members of the assembly praying out loud in tongues together. It may be that it is used in a designated group such as the cell group, house group or charismatic prayer group. Without such social support the use of the gift will inevitably diminish. In this way the practice of using the gift is given a concrete and publicly legitimated role. In churches where this does not take place then the gift will inevitably find itself on the margins and used in private devotion. Of course, the gift of speaking in tongues is not well understood and it may be that such public usage is threatening to those who do not understand it. In this case it is wise to remember the words of Paul again, 'If I speak in the tongues of men and of angels, but have not love, I am only a resounding gong or clanking symbol' (1 Cor 13.1, NIV). For love's sake, the gift may be marginalized to the realm of private devotion. But where there is understanding and appreciation there is to be found delightful expression.

For love's sake, the gift may be marginalized to the realm of private devotion

Private Devotion

Most people who speak in tongues do so within their own spiritual devotions. The gift can be used within a variety of spiritual traditions at points of preparation, adoration and intercession in ways that reflect the charismatic spirituality process often associated with worship services. Therefore it has been known to be used alongside liturgical prayer, contemplative exercises, adoration of the host (in Roman Catholicism and the Charismatic Episcopal Church) as well as Bible meditation and the traditional evangelical quiet time.

It is often the case that people use the gift while they go about their daily routines at work or at home. So while they wash the dishes, drive the car or prepare the dinner, people regularly use the gift to meet with the Lord and be nurtured by the Holy Spirit. As a gift of holy speech that comes from the spirit, it is possible to engage in a mundane activity while at the same time

The effect of such spiritual devotions within the life of the believer is to unite the holy with the profane

speak mysteries to the Lord. The effect of such spiritual devotions within the life of the believer is to unite the holy with the profane and demonstrate that the whole of life belongs to the Lord. In this regard this gift of the Spirit can become a spiritual resource for the Christian life.

Some Problems and Pitfalls

There are some problems and pitfalls associated with the gift of speaking in tongues that have less to do with the gift and more to do with sinful humanity. Nevertheless, these problems do occur and it is wise to be aware of them.

- **It can be associated with spiritual pride.** The mysterious quality of the gift means that it can be understood in a 'super' spiritual sense. Like the Corinthian charismatics it can be understood and used as a badge of superiority. Clearly, while Paul valued the gift, he emphasized that its value in the assembly was for the common good. If that could not be possible then it should be used in a personal and individual manner.

- **It can be overemphasized.** In a sense, this relates to the point above, but it can also be overemphasized by those who do not use it with pride as their motive. The spiritual life needs a balanced diet, to use the metaphor of nutrition, which includes rational engagement, communal practices, rituals and mystery. Tongues belong to a number of these items but must be understood to be secondary to the Scriptures, the intelligible communal life of worship and prayer and the sacramental life of the church.

- **It can be a boundary marker.** The classical Pentecostal denominations made it a boundary marker by linking it with a central doctrine (initial evidence of baptism in the Spirit). It therefore defines who is inside and who is outside a particular Christian group or denomination. There are many Pentecostals who no longer believe in this doctrine but cannot say so publicly. Similarly, in the 1960s and 1970s the charismatic renewal movement emphasized the gift as marking who was in and outside of the renewal movement. Thankfully, this is no longer the case, but it can still be used in this way.

- **It can be a stumbling block to outsiders.** Like the situation in Corinth, if it is used without due control within the public worship of the churches it can cause a scandal for those who misunderstand its nature and function. In this case, rather than being attracted to the gospel of Jesus Christ, there is a rejection of not only this gift but the grace of God. Therefore, care should be taken that this gift should not be seen to be a stumbling block. In the presence of unbelievers, the gift should be explained and interpreted to them.

- **It can be a mechanism of manipulation.** This particular pitfall is associated with the gift of interpretation. The gift of tongues and interpretation may be hijacked by powerful characters in the church who use it to influence others. Under the cloak of inspiration things can be said and claims made that are simply wrong. It is here that we note the words of Paul again, 'the spirits of the prophets are subject to the control of the prophets' (1 Cor 15.32). All interpretations should be weighed and assessed and policies should be put in place for leaders and others with 'discernment' to test the message or revelations.

All of these problems and pitfalls can be avoided by a proper understanding of the Christian life and in particular gospel priorities. The edification of the church is the primary aim of speaking in tongues and the sustenance of the Christian within the life of faith falls within this. To this end, the gift of speaking in tongues is truly from the Lord of the Spirit to be used by the human spirit for holy and mysterious speech to the praise and glory of God.

Questions for Reflection

- In the churches you know where the gift is practised, what would be the most common expression? Where and when and by whom?

- In the light of the problems identified, what guidelines might a church put in place to guard and guide its use?

7 Conclusion

The gift of speaking in tongues is one that is initiated and resourced by God himself as something of great benefit in the Christian life.

It is a gift of the *Holy Spirit* that is used by the *human spirit*. Without a desire and will to engage with this gift it will diminish like other abilities and capacities. Being sustained in a spirituality that is given expression within a community of faith, the church, it may be occasions of either miraculous or natural speech. It may, on occasions be the event of a miracle whereby a real and unlearned human language is spoken, but mostly it will be a language of the human spirit expressing Spirit inspired *mysteries*, like a groan or a cry unto God. As such, it is a symbol of divine-human encounter and means of Christian transformation within the kingdom of God. In this context it can be designated a sacrament, and like all sacraments it must be treated as *holy* unto the Lord. Thus it unites the Holy Spirit, the human spirit and the gift of holy speech in charismatic spirituality.

Further Reading

Further literature by the author on the subject of speaking in tongues, charismatic spirituality and theology include:

'The Future of Glossolalia: Fundamentalist or Experientialist?,' *Religion* 28 (1998) pp 233–244. A revised version appears as 'Glossolalia and Postmodernity' in *Practical Theology: Charismatic and Empirical Perspectives* (Carlisle: Paternoster, 2003) pp 131–155.

'The Socialization of Glossolalia' in Leslie J Francis (ed), *Sociology, Theology and the Curriculum* (London: Cassell, 1999) pp 125–134. A revised version appears as 'Glossolalia and Socialization' in *Practical Theology: Charismatic and Empirical Perspectives* (Carlisle: Paternoster, 2003) pp 215–229.

'The Symbolism of Charismatic Glossolalia,' *Journal of Empirical Theology* 12.1 (1999) pp 37–50.

'The Nature and Function of New Testament Glossolalia,' *Evangelical Quarterly* 72.7 (2000) pp 135–150.

Charismatic Glossolalia: an empirical-theological study (Aldershot: Ashgate, 2002).

'Practical Theology and Charismatic Spirituality: Dialectics in the Spirit,' *Journal of Pentecostal Theology* 10.2 (2002) pp 93–109.

'Affective Theological Praxis: Understanding the Direct Object of Practical Theology,' *International Journal of Practical Theology* 8.1 (2004) pp 34–52—includes a discussion of people's experiences of speaking in tongues.

'Charismatic Theology: Approaches and Themes,' *Journal of Beliefs and Values* 25.2 (2004) pp 177–190.

Editor, *Speaking in Tongues: Multidisciplinary Perspectives* (Carlisle: Paternoster, *forthcoming*, 2005/6).

Other books and articles on the subject include:

Gerald Hovenden, *Speaking in Tongues: The New Testament Evidence in Context* (Sheffield: Sheffield Academic Press, 2002).

Frank D Macchia, 'Sighs Too Deep for Words: Towards a Theology of Glossolalia,' *Journal of Pentecostal Theology* 1 (1992) pp 47–73.

Frank D Macchia, 'Tongues as a Sign: Towards a Sacramental Understanding of Pentecostal Experience,' *PNEUMA: The Journal of the Society for Pentecostal Studies* 15.1 (1993) pp 61–76.

H Newton Malony and A Adams Lovekin, *Glossolalia: Behavioural Science Perspectives on Speaking in Tongues* (New York: Oxford University Press, 1985).

Watson E Mills, *A Theological/Exegetical Approach to Glossolalia* (Lanham: University Press of America, 1985).

Watson E Mills (ed), *Speaking in Tongues: A Guide to Research on Glossolalia* (Grand Rapids: Eerdmans, 1986).

Max Turner, *The Holy Spirit and Spiritual Gifts Then and Now* (Carlisle: Paternoster, 1996).

Max Turner, 'Tongues: An Experience for All in the Pauline Churches?' *Asian Journal of Pentecostal Studies* 1.2 (1998) pp 231–253.

Notes

1   Reuben A Hartwick, 'Speaking in Tongues: The Initial Physical Evidence of the Baptism in the Holy Spirit,' *Paraclete* 29.3 (1995) pp 9–15 (p 9).

2   Michael Harper, *Walk in the Spirit* (London: Hodder & Stoughton, 1968) p 21.

3   Nigel Scotland, *Charismatics and the Next Millennium: Do They Have a Future?* (London: Hodder & Stoughton, 1995) pp 30–37.

4   The Jesus Prayer has a number of variations but the main version is: 'Lord Jesus Christ, Son of God, have mercy on me a sinner.' See Irma Zaleski, *Living the Jesus Prayer* (Leonminster: Novalis and Gracewing, 1997).

5   Gordon D Fee, *God's Empowering Presence: The Holy Spirit in the Letters of Paul* (Peabody MA: Hendrickson, 1994) pp 24–26.

6   Gordon D Fee, 'Toward a Pauline Theology of Glossolalia,' in Robert P Menzies and Wonsuk Ma (eds), *Pentecostalism in Context: Essays in Honour of William W Menzies* (Sheffield: Sheffield Academic Press, 1997) pp 24–37.

7   Simon Chan, 'The Language Game of Glossolalia, or Making Sense of the "Initial Evidence,"' in Robert P Menzies and Wonsuk Ma (eds), *Pentecostalism in Context: Essays in Honour of William W Menzies* (Sheffield: Sheffield Academic Press, 1997) pp 80–95.

8   John Calvin, *The Institutes of Christian Religion,* J T McNeill (ed) and F L Battles (trans) (Philadelphia: The Westminster Press) Vol 2, Book 4, chapter 14, paragraph 1.